Secrets of Driving and Automobile Care

Michael Ghatine

Secrets of Driving and Automobile Care by Michael Ghatine
Edited by Gary W Lund
Illustrations by Flanda Sargoni
Book design by Shirley Aguinaldo
Published by In Our Words Inc. (IOWI)

Library and Archives Canada Cataloguing in Publication

Ghatine, Michael, author
    Secrets of driving and automobile care / Michael Ghatine.

ISBN 978-1-926926-42-1 (pbk.)

    1. Automobile driving. 2. Automobiles--Maintenance and repair.
3. Traffic safety. I. Title.

TL152.5.G43 2014   629.28'3   C2014-904049-0

Copyright © 2013 Michael Ghatine

No part of this publication may be reproduced, stored in a retrieval system or transmitted in any form or by any means without the prior written permission of the author and publisher.

*"learn how to play chess
before you learn how to drive"*

~ Mike Ghatine

Contents

Introduction 6

Choosing a Car and Insurance 8
   Used Car Inspection Tips 10
   Insurance: the Cost of Traffic Tickets and Accidents 11

Prepare Yourself and Your Car Each Day 12
   Your Fitness to Drive 12
   Vehicle Inspection and Preparation 12

Principles of Safe Driving 18
   Stay in Control 18
   Avoid Distractions 19
   Don't Drive When Tired or Sleepy 21
   Keep Your Cool in a Traffic Jam 21
   Resist Road Rage 22

Safe and Effective Driving Techniques 24
   Freeway Driving 28
   What to Do when Pulled Over by Police 31
   Adapt to the Weather, Season, and Time of Day ... 32
   Driving Habits that Improve Fuel Efficiency 36

Collisions and Break-Downs 37
   What to Do after a Serious Collision 37
   What to Do if Your Vehicle Breaks Down 37
   What to Do If You Get a Flat Tire 39

Vehicle Repairs and Maintenance 40
   Tires 42
   Brakes 43
   Cooling System 45
   Oil Changes 46
   Battery 47
   Lights 48
   Cracked Windshield 48
   A Final Tip on Repairs and Maintenance 49

Conclusion 50

Introduction

I drive a transport truck for a living. Over many years of hauling, I've observed many examples of good driving habits as well as bad ones. People who take care of their vehicles and drive with skill and a professional attitude improve everyone's chances of getting to their destinations safely and on time.

I've also witnessed many incidents that resulted from poor driving habits and attitudes. These included near-misses, collisions, and roll-overs—sometimes with tragic results and long-term, painful, and costly consequences. They were all unnecessary; all avoidable.

I wrote this book to share with the motoring public, many things I've observed and learned over my years on the road, about safe driving practices and vehicle care. In the practice of driving, I follow the strategies used in playing chess. I believe that if you use the same tactics as those used when playing chess, it will make you a better driver. In the pages that follow, I will explain how applying some basic strategies of chess can help anyone be a better driver.

In addition to many years' experience as a professional driver, I am a qualified auto mechanic, and licensed driving instructor. I put the knowledge, experience and expertise gained in all these three driving-related professions together to write this handy guide on safe driving and auto care. The tips on basic vehicle maintenance, safety checks, and attentive driving, make this book useful for new as well as experienced drivers.

Disclaimer—This book is not a substitute for your vehicle owner's manual or for your provincial or state driver's manual, or licensing study manual. Nor is it intended to substitute for professional legal opinion. It consists of my observations and conclusions, based on my driving experience over many years.

Note on terminology—The terms car, truck, and vehicle are generally used interchangeably in this book.

Choosing a Car and Insurance

Congratulations—you've passed your driving test! Now it's time to choose a suitable car that meets your needs and budget. You'll need to sit down and calculate the costs associated with purchasing a car: the maintenance and fuel costs, as well as loan costs if you are financing the car. Some questions to ask yourself are:

- What kind of a car will suit me?
- Do I need four, six, or eight cylinders?
- Do I need two doors or four?
- Do I need the practicality of a family car or would I rather have the fun of a sports car?
- Should I buy a new car or a used car?
- Is it for business or pleasure?
- What will auto insurance cost?

Following the 'secrets' below can help lower your insurance rates:

1. Shop around and call a number of insurance companies and brokers to find the best deal.
2. If you drive a newer car, increase your deductibles.
3. If you drive an older car, remove collision coverage and comprehensive.
4. Keep your driving record clean! Any traffic ticket or claim—even if you were not at fault—may still increase your insurance premiums.
5. If possible, try not to involve the insurance company for minor claims; however, your insurance policy may state that you are required to report all accidents, regardless of the amount of damage.
6. If you get any traffic ticket, talk to a traffic lawyer or paralegal for advice.

USED CAR INSPECTION TIPS

When inspecting a used car – First, check the engine oil by pulling the oil dipstick; if the oil is creamy and white, the engine has major problems. Next, turn the ignition switch to the *on* position, and you will see some red and yellow lights on the instrument panel. These include the *Check Engine, ABS*, and *Air Bags* lights. Then when you start the engine, all the lights must go off; if they don't turn on or off as described, there is a major problem(s). (Exceptions: the *Parking Brake* light will remain on until the brake is released, and the *Fasten Seat Belt* light will stay on if the driver's seat belt is not fastened).

Look under the vehicle for any major oil or fluid leaks. With the engine running, stand behind the vehicle and have someone press on the throttle (gas pedal). If you see any smoke—blue, white or black—there is a problem with the engine. Take the vehicle for a road test and drive the vehicle the way you are going to drive every day. Make sure the transmission shifts gears smoothly, and the vehicle is not pulling to the right or left. If the engine has recently been washed, polished, or the oil has been changed, it's not a good sign, because the seller may be trying to hide evidence of leaks or internal engine trouble. At the end, before buying, if you are not sure that it's a good vehicle, take it to a mechanic's shop for an inspection, and also make sure there is no lien (debt) against the vehicle.

INSURANCE: THE COST OF TRAFFIC TICKETS AND ACCIDENTS

Traffic tickets, collisions, and any claims are costly. That includes insurance deductibles, fines and downtime, which can be thousands of dollars. There is another surprising cost as a consequence, which is higher insurance rates, and you will find that out when it's time to renew your insurance. Most insurance companies will look at your insurance history, accidents, tickets and any claims even if you are not at fault, to determine the rate they offer you. That is why it's very important to keep your driving history free of accidents, traffic tickets, and any claim (e.g., breaking in to your car, minor scratches or dent repair, windshield chip and crack repair), in order to maintain a lower insurance rate.

Prepare Yourself and Your Car Each Day

YOUR FITNESS TO DRIVE

Now that you have your driver's license, a car, and insurance, make the following checkpoints your daily habit. Before you start driving, ask yourself:

- Do I feel comfortable to drive alone, or do I need to drive with an experienced driver?

- How well do I know the rules of the road, and what is my driver's licence restriction, if any?

- If I am required to wear prescription glasses, am I wearing them, or if I take medication on a daily basis, do I have it with me?

VEHICLE INSPECTION AND PREPARATION

Exterior inspection

If you feel you are ready to drive, then it's time to inspect your vehicle. With the engine off, raise the hood and then check the engine oil, power steering fluid, brake fluid (check brake fluid without removing the filler cap—it is visible through a transparent window in the reservoir), windshield washer fluid, and radiator fluid (engine coolant). If all is okay, close the hood gently but firmly (slamming the hood could damage the hood or headlights.)

Then do a circle-check around the vehicle with all the lights and four-way flashers on. Walk around the vehicle; check all the lights, look under the car for any fluid leaks (fuel, transmission fluid, radiator fluid, or engine oil). Check tire condition and inflation using a tire air-pressure gauge if possible. Also check the spare tire air pressure, look for any loose objects on or around the vehicle, and wash or wipe the windows and mirrors, cleaning off any snow or dirt. Dirty windows not only obscure visibility but can increase glare and reflections.

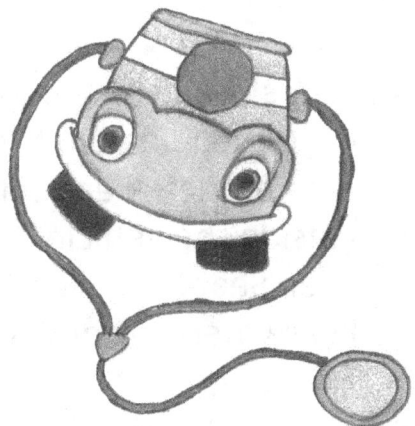

Interior inspection and adjustments

Inside the vehicle, check that all documents are present (vehicle registration, insurance, and driver's licence). Clean and wipe all the windows and remove any objects that obscure the view, including any that are hanging on the rear view mirror or on top of the dashboard or back window shelf. Make sure everything is secured. Adjust mirrors, buckle and adjust your seat belt.

Note: If you have passengers on board, remember that you are in charge of operating the vehicle, and responsible for its safe operation, and the safety of your passengers, so you must be comfortable when driving. Therefore, adjust the cabin temperature for your comfort not the passengers'; don't pull the seat close to the steering wheel for the comfort of the passenger behind you.

With the ignition on, check all gauges—especially the fuel gauge, making sure there is enough fuel for your trip.

Safety equipment must be used – Driver and passengers must have their seat belts on at all times when the vehicle is in motion. Seat belts will keep all the passengers inside the vehicle in the event of a collision or roll-over. Seat belts significantly reduce injuries and save lives when motor vehicle collisions occur.

The driver is responsible for ensuring that passengers under 16 years of age are wearing their seat belts. Use a proper child car seat for children and always place them on the back seat.

Plan, avoid distractions, and stay alert – Always prepare for an alternative route in case of road closure, accident, or traffic jam. Plan your trip ahead of time.

Make sure you are familiar with all the controls in your vehicle before you start driving.

You don't need any distractions when you drive, so before you put the car in gear, take care of any personal things like phone calls; and set the GPS and your favorite radio station.

A little fresh air can work wonders, so always keep your window cracked open for fresh air. This will also prevent carbon monoxide from penetrating the cabin in the case of an exhaust leak.

Every second counts; keep your hands on the wheel and eyes on the road at all times. Remember, distraction kills.

Always clean the windshield outside and inside. Windshields do get dirty from the inside. Smoking, breathing, and damp clothing will create a fog or film on the windshield. A dirty windshield will significantly impair your ability to see, and make your eyes tired. Keep the floor inside of your vehicle dry; a wet floor will steam and cause fog. In winter, use winter or rubber floor mats only and keep them free of snow and water.

Asphalt contains oil, and when roads are wet, oil at the surface mixes with the water, and this oily liquid splashes onto the windshield. It can smear, and obscure your vision. Whenever fueling the car at a gas station, wash the windows outside and inside, and wipe the windshield-wiper blades monthly with an alcohol wipe. In summer (not in winter), mix some glass cleaner such as Windex into the vehicle windshield-washer fluid reservoir, which will help remove grease that sticks to the windshield and wiper blades. Wash windows and windshield regularly by using a squeegee and glass cleaner. Cleaning the windshield and wiper blades is one of the least expensive yet most effective things you can do to enhance your driving safety and ease. Replace wiper blades at least once a year. Remember, if you can't see, you can't drive!

Cold weather vehicle preparation

On cold days, warm up your vehicle and defrost the windshield by using a remote starter while you wait inside your home or workplace in comfort. Don't just start the car and drive without warming the vehicle or cleaning the windows. Taking a few minutes for this can save you thousands of dollars in vehicle damage and down time. At the beginning of driving on a cold day, for proper performance of the vehicle, drive slowly to allow the engine, transmission, differential, and tires to warm up gradually. Many accidents happen at the beginning of the trip when tires are cold. Tires are made from rubber, and in cold temperature when the vehicle is parked over a period of time, rubber gets stiff and loses some of its grip. By allowing some time and driving slowly, the tires will warm up and have better grip.

If your vehicle is equipped with an engine block heater, make sure to plug it in when the temperature is below freezing. This will keep the engine warm and save the engine gaskets from cracking and protect oil from freezing. When you start the engine, the engine temperature rises rapidly from extremely cold to extremely hot, and this sudden change can cause the gaskets to deteriorate (engine and gasket will contract and expand), resulting in an oil leak.

Principles of Safe Driving

STAY IN CONTROL

Be in control of your vehicle at all times – Most vehicles are built to go faster than the speed limit on freeways—some up to 200 km/h (124 mph). But we all know there is no freeway in North America where it's legal to drive as fast as most vehicles can go, so one wonders why cars are made to go that fast? Let's be responsible and stay in control. Drive like a professional and with confidence.

Drive like you're playing chess; if you know the strategies of chess in addition to the rules of the game, then most likely you can be a good and safe driver. Here are some strategies of chess adapted as appropriate for driving:

1. Have a plan.
2. Keep the noise and other distractions inside the vehicle to a minimum.
3. Pay attention to driving.
4. Plan your moves ahead of time.
5. Be prepared, and don't panic but stay calm in the event of other drivers' unexpected moves.
6. Be road-ready and keep your eyes moving.

7. The most common errors are preventable, simple mistakes that you make on a daily basis. They can cost time, money, and sometimes a life.

8. Remember driving a vehicle is not a game, but a serious responsibility, and a small mistake can change a life. Be a responsible driver.

AVOID DISTRACTIONS

What are distractions? Distractions include adjusting the radio, changing CDs, texting, eating, smoking, looking for a street address, daydreaming, reaching for items inside the vehicle, personal grooming tasks and putting on makeup, looking over the shoulders at an accident scene or other things, and talking to passengers or on a cell phone—even with a hands-free device. Distractions also include driving as part of a convoy (two or more cars) and dangerous activities like chasing each other.

With distractions, driving performance is significantly compromised, because it's hard to concentrate on two things at the same time, especially for new or inexperienced drivers.

Avoid Distractions and Impairment – Minimize conversations with passengers, and especially, don't get into complicated or heated conversations. You are more likely to have a crash when you're distracted while driving.

Be 100 percent alert and focused on your driving. Nervous or angry? Don't bring it into the car with you—take a few minutes to cool down before stepping into the vehicle.

When driving and feeling nervous, pull over and take a break, stretch, and do some deep breathing; then resume driving when ready. Daydreaming behind the wheel can lead to a nightmare—an accident and its consequences. Stay alert and stay alive. It all starts with a good sleep to avoid fatigue.

Never drive if impaired by alcohol, drugs, fatigue, or stress. No one can assume that it's safe to drive after consuming a beer, glass of wine, or any amount of alcohol—every person has a different limit in alcohol tolerance. The best way to avoid an accident due to drinking and driving is not to drink at all. The consequences could be losing your driver's licence, paying hefty fines, increased insurance costs, going to jail, or in the worst case scenario causing loss of life. Mixing certain drugs with driving has the same effect as mixing alcohol with driving; either way, your ability to function will be impaired. Avoid medication that causes drowsiness before or when driving.

Drive Defensively and Pro-actively – Don't drive along with other vehicles—especially large vehicles—and keep the area around your vehicle clear for emergency manoeuvres.

Be road ready (and ready for adversity such as bad weather, collision, or break-down), and if possible avoid driving during rush hours, bad weather, under stress, or at night.

DON'T DRIVE WHEN TIRED OR SLEEPY

One way to avoid fatigue is to alternate the route you take when driving to work and back. Try different roads to keep yourself alert. Staying with the same route every day can lead to fatigue and day-dreaming. But on any trip, if you do find you are feeling tired or sleepy, don't fight the fatigue. No matter how close you are to your destination, pull over and park in a safe spot, and take a nap, even if only for a few minutes. By sacrificing a few minutes, you may be saving yourself from years of problems, grief, and regret—you may even save your life or another's. Better to arrive late than never.

KEEP YOUR COOL IN A TRAFFIC JAM

If it is your daily routine to drive during rush hours, you must be prepared for and not surprised by delays. If you look around you and see that everyone else is stuck in the traffic, you'll see that there is no point in driving aggressively and carelessly. Be patient. In heavy traffic, jockeying for a better position won't help. Just choose a lane and stay in it; every lane change just puts you in greater risk of a collision. Listen to soothing music that you like, and relax. Listen to traffic reports. If you hear of trouble ahead, (e.g. accidents, construction), aim for a different route. Get off the freeway; use a global positioning system (GPS) to navigate your way around the blockage. (Don't install a GPS on the top of the instrument panel where it could obstruct the view through the windshield. Use voice commands on your GPS when possible.)

RESIST ROAD RAGE

Remain calm and in a positive frame of mind. Slow down and relax. Most importantly, reduce driving stress by allowing more than enough time to get where you are going. That extra time will get you to your destination safe and stress-free. To help get you out the door earlier, adjust your alarm clock 15 minutes ahead of the real time.

Remember the three P's: practice, patience and be polite. You can't control the way others drive but you can control your own driving. Drive professionally and safely. Motorists need to guard against road rage. It's like an avalanche, and no good comes from it. Don't retaliate. Never take another driver's acts personally. Don't provoke the other driver by making any hand gestures, honking the horn or cutting him/her off. Slow down or pull over and ask yourself, "Is getting back at that person worth my time or life? Am I acting professionally? Is that the only bad driver on the road? Do I want to go home tonight?" Be polite and courteous, even when others are not. Back off, keep a safe distance, and keep your energy for more important things. Bad drivers will get their due sooner or later. Never put yourself or others in danger. If you are harassed by another driver and being followed, do not go home. Call police or go to the nearest police station.

Safe and Effective Driving Techniques

After the checks and adjustments, and if you feel you are ready to drive, start the motor. With your right foot on the brake pedal, put the transmission in *Drive* and release the emergency brake. Check mirrors, look over your shoulders to check your blind spots, and when clear, signal your intention to move into the driving lane. Don't forget to turn the signal light off, and check the rear-view mirror again. Pay attention to traffic signs (speed limit, stop signs, school zones, turns, one-way streets); it could save your life as well as others'.

Take weather and road conditions into consideration. Drive according to the road conditions; slow down in bad weather, construction and school zones. Watch for pedestrians, bikes, and kids. When approaching a stop sign, always check under the main stop sign to see if it's marked as a 4-way or 2-way stop. Drive at the same speed as the traffic around you within the speed limits.

Don't zigzag in traffic—you will end up behind another slow-moving vehicle anyway. Dangerous operation of a motor vehicle is a serious offence, punishable by law. Some examples are excessive speeding (especially in a school or construction zone), and driving too fast for the road conditions, such as on a snow-covered road.

Drive at a speed that allows you to stop safely – The posted speed limit applies only when the road is in good condition (sunny, clear, dry, and no construction). In poor conditions, drive below the posted speed limit. Driving too fast when road conditions are bad is very risky, and may result in a collision or loss of control of the vehicle. Remember to stay in the right lane and reserve the left lane for passing only. Check mirrors and use signals before changing lanes. Check mirrors every few seconds to know what's around you.

Always look well ahead of the vehicle in front of you, and keep a safe distance. If you see brake lights or traffic stopped ahead of you, apply the brake lightly to inform the drivers behind you that you're about to slow down or stop. Always communicate with vehicles around you by using signals and brake lights. If you see an emergency vehicle, stay cool. React quickly and calmly; do not slam on the brake to stop in the middle of the road, or pull over suddenly. Check mirrors, signal, and check your blind spot. If safe, pull over to the right side of the roadway and stop until the emergency vehicle passes; then check mirrors, signal, and when safe, pull out, and continue driving. Keep your eyes moving.

When driving in the city, always watch for pedestrians. They can be especially careless when they are trying to catch a bus or taxi. With their eyes on the bus, they may start crossing the street, or start running to catch the bus without paying attention to the traffic around them. Pedestrians may be blinded with their hoods pulled partially over their faces in winter, and many wear headphones tuned into their MP3 players or cell phones, instead of paying attention to the traffic around them. At intersections marked with stop signs, don't just slow down or make a rolling stop. Come to a full stop, look left and right, watch for cars, bikes, and pedestrians. Don't rush. Pay special attention at intersections when it is raining and at night. Rain and darkness make pedestrians much more difficult to spot. Watch for children in residential areas; they may dart into the road from between the parked cars. Use your horn only for getting the attention of other drivers or pedestrians, not to make a suggestion or for scolding others. Before crossing railroad tracks, look, listen—and live.

Use waiting time to observe – When stopped at intersections, don't just look straight at the traffic light while waiting for the green light, or distract yourself by doing anything but pay attention to driving. Look and observe the area around you, and make sure the way ahead is clear. When the light turns green, proceed with caution. Before crossing the intersection, start out slowly, checking both left and right; watch for emergency vehicles, pedestrians, or bikes that may still be crossing. When making turns at intersections, check your path for pedestrians. You don't want to get stuck in the middle of the intersection, waiting for pedestrians to cross. Check for parked cars, break-downs, or accidents. Always observe and look around. When you are making a left turn at an intersection and the light is turning yellow or red, watch for oncoming cars—don't proceed just because the light is changing—make sure oncoming cars stop or pass by before making the left turn. The oncoming car might run the red light because they are blinded by the sun, drunk, in a rush, or simply don't want to stop. If you are turning left at an intersection and see that an oncoming vehicle is signaling to turn left or right, don't automatically proceed on the assumption that the driver intends to turn. The driver may have forgotten to cancel the turn signal. So be sure the oncoming vehicle is actually turning (or wait for it to pass) before you proceed.

Avoid tailgating by staying well back. It is not the car crash that kills you; it is your violent collision with your car's interior that causes injuries. Following too closely is the number one driver action that results in collisions. Don't follow too close to the vehicle in front; by doing that you will save your tires, brakes, and maybe your life. When tailgating, your sudden stops in stop-and-go traffic will over-heat the brakes and make them less responsive. Tailgating will not get you to your destination any sooner, rather it may get you into a collision and higher insurance rates sooner.

FREEWAY DRIVING

When entering a freeway, you must enter safely and smoothly, without slowing down other vehicles. Adjust your speed to the traffic while you are still on the ramp. Most ramps are long enough to give you enough time to accelerate to match the traffic speed on the freeway.

When driving on a freeway, following closely is dangerous, so keep a safe distance. Look well ahead and check mirrors, and remember to drive in the right lane and keep the left lane open for passing (it's the law). It's also the law to stay within the speed limit, but even so, you should not block faster traffic.

When moving at high speed, it's dangerous to make sudden swerves, so if you suddenly come upon stopped traffic or an accident scene, first brake hard, before steering into a clear lane or space. If you are about to miss your exit, don't attempt to exit by suddenly making an unsafe lane change, or by backing up on the freeway. Continue to the next exit and turn around; it will likely take only a few extra minutes, which is far better than risking a crash. Always know where you are: pay attention to surroundings and take note of the most recent town, exit, or street in case you need to call for emergency help.

When changing lanes, let other drivers know your intentions ahead of time—signal a lane change *before* you move over, not just *as* you move over. Check the rear view and side mirrors, shoulder-check the blind spot, then move over when it's safe. If you need to move over more than one lane, change only one lane at a time, cancelling the signal after each lane change. Changing lanes suddenly on icy or snowy roads can send your vehicle into a spin. To avoid this, reduce your speed (if that doesn't interfere with the traffic flow), and steer gently to change lanes. Be prepared to recover from a spin or loss of vehicle control.

Stay clear of large vehicles – Large vehicles take longer to come to a complete stop. Give them extra space on all sides. Avoid staying in a large vehicle's blind spot. Its driver may not see you, and may attempt a quick lane change to avoid suddenly stopped traffic ahead, and sideswipe your vehicle. When driving behind a large vehicle, pay attention to its tail lights. If you are approaching one from behind, note especially if the four-way hazard warning lights are flashing. This may indicate that the truck is stopped or backing up. Maintain a safe following distance—remember, if you can't see the vehicle's mirrors, the driver can't see you. Watch for flying objects coming off large vehicles (ice or snow from the top of the vehicle, stones from their wheels, and even dislodged vehicle parts).

WHAT TO DO WHEN PULLED OVER BY POLICE

When a police officer is signalling you to pull over, stay calm. Check mirrors, signal, check your blind spot, then move to the right side of the road, stop, put the transmission in park, and apply the parking brake. Switch on the four-way hazard warning lights, and then roll your window down. If you're stopped at night, turn on the interior light as well. Keep both your hands on the steering wheel and wait for the officer's instruction. Don't make sudden moves, and be prepared to hand over your driver's licence, insurance, and vehicle registration. Answer only what you are asked, and be polite: use respectful language such as "yes sir" and "no officer." When you are asked if you know why you have been pulled over; just respond, "No, officer, I do not know why." Anything you say may be recorded and it could be used against you in court.

ADAPT TO THE WEATHER, SEASON, AND TIME OF DAY

Overconfidence in four-wheel drive is deadly

When driving on slippery roads use caution, especially when driving a 4x4 vehicle. All vehicles need traction for moving ahead and accelerating, steering, and braking. Four-wheel drive vehicles *do* have more traction for propulsion, to pull a vehicle through deep snow or mud. But they have the same braking system as two-wheel drive vehicles, so they don't stop any faster than other vehicles. Both 2WD and 4WD vehicles depend on the tires maintaining grip on the road for effective steering.

Most drivers of 4WD vehicles think they can drive faster than 2WDs, so many of them do drive faster. But when it comes to stopping and negotiating curves, they realize too late that they are going too fast. That is why there are more roll-overs and other accidents with 4WD vehicles on slippery roads.

When driving in snow or rain, at the beginning of driving do some testing by braking to find out how slippery the roads are, so you will have an idea how fast you can go and how much space you need around you. Make sure every once in a while to do light braking to keep the brake pads and rotors dry so when you want to make the actual stop the brakes pads and rotors will be dry and ready.

If you lose control of your vehicle on a slippery road, don't panic; don't step hard on the brake pedal, or freeze behind the wheel. Instead, brake lightly, look where you want to go, and steer the vehicle in that direction. Be nimble and calm, turning the steering to the left or right as needed. Don't over-steer. On snow, the vehicle's reaction to steering input may be delayed, leading you to over-steer. The result can be an overcorrection and a skid in the opposite direction from the first skid.

Find a roomy place where it's safe to practise getting out of skids, so you will be prepared when the skill is needed. If you are driving when rainfall begins, slow down and drive with caution. Asphalt and other paved surfaces contain oils in their mixtures. The road seeps oil to the surface, and more so in warmer weather. As the rain begins to accumulate on the road, the water mixes with the oil, creating a slick surface, and tires lose grip. This is why many accidents happen at the beginning of a rainfall. Hydroplaning is another danger when driving in the rain. When driving too fast for the wet conditions, tires may lose contact with the pavement, and you lose control of the vehicle. Always drive according to road conditions.

Your vehicle is most likely equipped with an automatic transmission. Next to the transmission control lever is an indicator that points to the transmission gear currently selected. It indicates

Park, Reverse, Neutral, Overdrive, D3, D2, and D1 (or similar). Have you used all of the available gears? Check with your dealer or owner's manual for the proper use of a transmission on slippery roads.

What to do if stuck in the snow – Don't just put the transmission in drive or first gear and spin the wheels. Especially if the temperature is near the freezing mark, spinning the wheels will make matters worse by creating a slick layer of melted snow, which may also turn to ice. Spinning the tires will only make it more difficult to get out of the situation.

With a manual transmission, choose second gear to minimize tire spinning, then rock the vehicle back and forth by slowly releasing and pressing the clutch without spinning the wheels. The rocking motion should create enough momentum to move the vehicle out of its rut.

The process will be a bit different for automatic transmissions. To create the same effect with an automatic transmission, use both feet: one on the throttle (gas pedal) and the other on the brake. Place the transmission in Drive (D) and slightly push on the throttle and then release the brake. When the vehicle stops moving forward, release the throttle and then apply brakes, select reverse, slightly press the throttle and then release the brake; the idea is to rock the vehicle back and forth without spinning the wheels. It's a good idea to carry a bag of sand in the trunk. Placing some sand just ahead of and behind the tire with the least traction (the tire that is spinning) may provide enough traction to get you out of the rut.

Note: Many automatics will always start out in the lowest gear regardless of shift-selector placement. But with some, if you position the shift selector to 2nd gear (D2) you can start out in 2nd, which, as with manual transmissions, is a taller gear than 1st, and less likely to spin. Choose D2 if your vehicle will begin there; otherwise, use (D) for the forward gear.

Driving at night

Make your vehicle visible to others by keeping the lights on whenever the vehicle is moving.

When driving at night towards an oncoming vehicle with its high beams on, do not look directly into the headlights; try to ignore the glare and look straight ahead or slightly to the right.

Don't use high beam headlights in snow or foggy conditions. High beams reflect the falling snow or the fog, making it harder to see the road and other vehicles. Reduce speed. If visibility is extremely poor, it's unsafe to drive. Pull over off the road where and when it is safe to do so, then relax and wait for conditions to improve. Bad weather usually won't last long.

DRIVING HABITS THAT IMPROVE FUEL EFFICIENCY

Eliminate unnecessary idling, and bad driving habits such as excessive speed and jack-rabbit starts. Be sure to have the correct tire size and type, and maintain proper tire inflation. If the radiator coolant level is low, if the air conditioning is running constantly, or if the vehicle's steering is out of alignment (you'll know because you are constantly fighting the steering wheel to keep the vehicle in a straight line)—all this will cause the engine to burn more fuel.

Collisions and Break-Downs

Accidents are preventable, and a collision or rollover is only an attitude away. If you are involved in a minor collision, do not stand between two vehicles in the middle of the road to exchange information. It is very dangerous and you can be crushed if another vehicle comes along and crashes into either your or the other damaged vehicle. First, take some pictures of the accident scene if you can do so safely, then move the vehicles to a safe place, if possible, and then exchange information.

WHAT TO DO AFTER A SERIOUS COLLISION

Stay calm. Turn off the engine, and turn hazards lights on, unlock the doors, and check for injuries. Call 911 for an ambulance or police. Use your cell phone camera or any other camera and take as many pictures as possible, from a safe position.

WHAT TO DO IF YOUR VEHICLE BREAKS DOWN

If your vehicle breaks down as you are driving, stay calm. Signal a lane-change and pull over to the shoulder if at all possible (don't let the vehicle stop in the middle of a driving lane). Once stopped, it's usually safer to stay inside the vehicle, but scan the surroundings for hazards, and judge for yourself where it is safe to stop. If you can, park in a slightly angled position, with the front of vehicle closer to the curb than the back wheel. If your car is hit from behind by another car, it will have less impact on you and your vehicle. On busy roads, don't try to flag down other vehicles. That will distract other drivers and may cause a collision. Lock the doors and call for help. Stay on the phone with someone.

Try to write down the license plate numbers of some of the cars driving by. If police need a witness to your incident, you will have a list of some people who passed by you and your car at that time. If you have to abandon your car, don't leave any personal belongings in the vehicle, or at least keep them out of sight. Remember, if there is nothing to see, there is nothing to steal. When help comes, phone someone you know and give a description of the car and the person helping you, even if that help is a tow truck or taxi. If you don't have a phone, leave a note in your car. Keep spare fuses in the glove box. In some cases, all it takes is a fuse to start your car and put you back on the road. Compare that to a tow to a repair shop, followed by a large bill. Keep emergency supplies in your vehicle, too. These include a blanket, lighter, candle, bottle of water, hard candy, and magnetic spare key holder (with key, under the car).

WHAT TO DO IF YOU GET A FLAT TIRE

Know where your spare tire is located. Keep it properly inflated and ready to be used in case of a flat tire. When driving, keep both hands on the steering wheel; if a tire gets a blowout, you'll have a better chance of maintaining control. Don't brake hard; just stay calm, smoothly release the throttle, and slow down gently. Don't stop your vehicle in an unsafe traffic lane where traffic is moving around you. Activate the four-way hazard lights, and move over to a safe place away from moving traffic even if you think the tire is going to be further damaged. It is possible to replace a tire but not a life; always practise safety first.

Note: Always carry tire repair kits and air compressor in your vehicle. Ask a tire shop technician how to use a tire repair kit in an emergency.

Vehicle Repairs and Maintenance

Severe Driving Conditions – When we hear "severe," we think of snow storms, freezing rain, heavy rain and fog, but there are other severe conditions we face every day and yet we don't consider it. Severe conditions include: driving in the city, heavy traffic, driving in extreme cold or heat, and driving on dirt or gravel roads. Vehicles driven in severe conditions require more frequent servicing. That includes oil changes, brake service, front end service, shocks, tires, and tune-ups. Don't forget the cabin air filter: a clogged cabin air filter will make the A/C and heater less efficient. Changing the cabin air filter once a year is recommended.

Shop Around for Repairs – When your vehicle needs repairs or maintenance, shop around. Don't accept just one mechanic's opinion; phone some alternative auto shops, describe the problem, and ask for an estimate so you will have an idea of the repair costs. If there is a major problem with the engine or transmission, you should have it repaired at a dealership, not by just any mechanic, because most non-dealer mechanics don't have the exact tools or training to properly rebuild complicated, major components. In some cases it's better to install a good used engine and transmission rather than rebuilding damaged ones.

The advantage of making prompt repairs – A car breaking down in the middle of the road can be costly and stressful. A trip to your mechanic when you first notice any unusual noise or action when driving (e.g., when turning or braking), could decrease the chance of your car breaking down, and your disappointment and frustration when you most need your car.

Tip: If the *Check Engine* light comes on, replace the gas tank cap. This is the most common cause, and this inexpensive part might fix the problem.

Keep your vehicle properly tuned – A simple tune up will save you thousands of dollars over time, simply by replacing spark plugs, fuel filter, air filter, and a faulty oxygen sensor. A periodic check at the shop will help ensure your car receives preventive measures and early intervention.

Prepare your vehicle for winter – As you pull out your winter coat, sweaters, and winter boots when cold weather arrives, consider the same winter preparations for your vehicle. Before temperatures start to drop, there are a few things that your car requires: oil change, coolant check, new sets of wiper blades, an extra jug of windshield washer fluid, bags of salt or sand, and most important— winter tires. Summer tires are made from stiff rubber to resist wear; in cold temperatures, summer tires get stiffer, and consequently because the roads are cold and hard, this means loss of traction. It is like rubbing two rocks against each other. Winter tires are made from a softer compound that resists stiffening, and creates better traction and handling. Remember to remove winter tires as soon as warm weather arrives, because winter tires are soft, they wear out more quickly. Ask your tire supplier about the benefits of winter and summer tires.

TIRES

Do not miss-match or install different tires on your vehicle other than what the vehicle's manufacturer recommends. Check the owner's manual or driver's door panel for proper tire size and air pressure. Make sure all tires installed on the vehicle are the same brand, type, tread, and size. If miss-matched tires are installed, you may not notice any difference in day to day driving, but with any unusual actions, such as swerving, turning sharply or braking suddenly, you may lose control of the vehicle.

Tire Maintenance – Properly inflated tires will improve fuel efficiency and extend tire life. Vehicles with under-inflated tires are more prone to loss of control and resultant crashes. Tires are one of the most important components of a vehicle, since they are the only connection between the vehicle and the road. Together with the brake system, they are the only components that can stop your vehicle.

How to find out the recommended tire pressure?
The maximum tire pressure is written on the tire sidewall, and refers to the pressure required to carry the maximum load of the tire. To find out the recommended tire pressure for your vehicle, refer to the information label, which is usually located on the edge of the driver's door or the door post; or refer to the owner's manual.

Also check the age of tires, whether those already on your vehicle, or if you are buying new or used tires. Even if the tire looks brand new it could be dry, and may crack or blow out when driving. Look on the sidewall of the tire for the letters D O T, followed by a four-digit code. The first two numbers are the week and last two numbers are the year in which the tire was manufactured. Tires age as well as wear, so fresher tires are better. Some guides recommend replacing any tires over 10 years old, as they may be unsafe.

Practice scheduled tire rotation to extend tire life. Move the tires to different positions on the car; front to the back and back to the front, every 15,000 km (10,000 miles). This practice helps the tires to wear evenly and last longer.

BRAKES

Time for brake service — When you hear a squealing noise during breaking, it means that your car's brake pads are almost worn down. The squeal comes from an indicator installed on the brake pads to warn the driver it's time for brake service. If you hear this squeal, have the brakes inspected soon to avoid damage to the rotors or losing your brakes. Other signs to watch for are longer stopping distances or low brake fluid. Make sure the parking brake (emergency brake) is in working condition. It should be applied any time the vehicle is parked. Such frequent use will help keep it from seizing. With automatic transmissions, put the transmission into park with the service brake applied, and then apply the parking brake before releasing the service brake. Now the parking brake will be holding the vehicle, and that will take the tension from the transmission.

The brake fluid in your vehicle is stored in the engine bay (under the hood), in a plastic reservoir (metal in older cars). The plastic containers are transparent so you can see the fluid level without having to remove the cap and look inside. Try to avoid removing the cap, to prevent the brake fluid from becoming contaminated with moisture or debris. Brake fluid is highly susceptible to absorbing moisture. When applying the brakes while the wheels are in motion, a tremendous amount of heat is transferred from the brake pads and rotors to the brake fluid. Even a small amount of moisture in the brake fluid could reduce braking effectiveness.

Water has different properties than brake fluid, and behaves differently with temperature changes. Every two years a brake fluid flush is recommended. Keep in mind—if you've done a complete brake service and are still having braking problems, then consider a brake fluid flush.

COOLING SYSTEM

Cooling system flush before winter – Engine coolant (antifreeze) dissipates heat and prevents freezing at low temperatures. With age, coolant deteriorates and becomes contaminated, and will be less effective at protecting your engine. If it loses its effectiveness as antifreeze, it may expand in very cold weather, and damage the engine or radiator directly. If it becomes less effective as a coolant, the engine may overheat in use, and be damaged. So it's important to ensure that the coolant is ready for any weather. Consider a radiator flush to clean out any buildup that might clog the vehicle's cooling system.

Never use water to top up the radiator or windshield washer reservoir; water will cause rust, which can clog up the cooling system. And unlike water, antifreeze won't expand and damage the engine. Engine coolant and windshield washer fluid are chemical compounds that have a much lower freezing point than water.

OIL CHANGES

How important are oil changes? Oil is like a car's blood; it prevents metal parts in your engine from grinding against each other, and also helps cool down the combustion chamber. Engine oil should be changed about every 5,000 miles (8,000 km) under normal driving conditions. If you usually drive in city traffic, stop-and-go traffic jams or very hilly terrain, then the oil must be changed more often. You can check the oil by pulling out the oil dipstick and rubbing a little oil between two fingers to test it. If it is not sticky, or if it's dark in color, then it's time for an oil change. An oil change just before winter helps your engine perform more efficiently. In the winter, thinner oil is recommended. Thick oil in cold temperatures gets extremely thick, and can make it difficult for the engine to start. It is important to make sure the oil grade matches the vehicle's owner-manual recommendation. When changing oil on older cars with high mileage, consider adding Lucas or a similar oil additive. Most truckers use such additives to help extend engine life. Don't forget to record the date and mileage when the oil change is done. When at your mechanic's shop for the oil change, ask for a brake and front end inspection. Many road accidents occur because of loose or damaged front end parts. We often hear on the news of a vehicle that left the road and crashed for unknown reasons. An inspection is the best way to prevent such incidents.

BATTERY

Monitor your battery's condition – Cold temperatures decrease battery power, making it harder to start an engine. Battery problems result from, for example, draining the battery by running lights for periods of time with the engine off, especially during times of extremely cold or hot temperatures. The alternator also plays an important role. An overcharging or undercharging alternator can cause permanent damage to the vehicle's battery. Fortunately, it is easy to detect problems in this area. First, if the red battery light on the instrument panel comes on while the engine is running, you will know there are battery or charging problems. Second, a good battery should start the car after a few hours rest after you've shut off those lights you had left on. A good battery should start strong in cold temperatures, as in warm temperatures.

Before winter, it's a good time to charge your battery using an automotive battery charger and schedule a check-up by a qualified mechanic to find out if the charging system or the old battery could cause any problems. In cold temperatures, keep the battery warm using fireproof insulations.

LIGHTS

Lights can save your life if they are working properly. For example, brake lights are the clearest, most attention-getting way to let a driver behind you know that your vehicle is quickly slowing down, stopping, or has stopped.

Check your vehicle's lights regularly. Make sure all lights are working, and that the headlights are aimed properly. The simplest way to check the lights is when you can see the reflection of the front lights on the glass windows of a store when you are parked in front of it. You can use the same technique with the rear lights if you back up towards a window. You can check the left and right brake lights, the centre brake light, turn signals, and reverse lights.

Be watching for another clue that indicates a burned out signal light: the signal indicator in the instrument panel blinks faster on one side than the other side.

If the headlights have become dull, cloudy, or yellowed, use a sponge and engine oil to polish the lens, or you can use headlight lens cleaner, which is available at any auto parts store.

CRACKED WINDSHIELD

In most cases it's better to replace a cracked or chipped windshield rather than repair it. The front windshield in time suffers all kinds of scratches and tiny chips from sand, rocks, ice, and wipers, all of which reduces visibility. So rather than fixing old glass, it's better to replace it with new, clear glass. In most cases the difference between replacing and repairing is not much. Do some comparison shopping and compare estimates to get the best deal.

A FINAL TIP ON REPAIRS AND MAINTENANCE

Rely on specialists. If you need your windshield repaired or changed, take your vehicle to an auto glass shop. If you need your transmission serviced, go to a shop where they only work on transmissions. If you need an exhaust system repair, go to a muffler shop. If you have electrical problems (e.g., starter, alternator), take your vehicle to a mechanic who specializes in electrical works. If you need a cooling system repair (radiator) take your vehicle to a service that does radiator repairs only. And if you need brake service, take your vehicle to a brake specialist.

You'll see a pattern in the above advice. With specialized services, you will usually get a better price for the parts and labour, and you will be dealing with someone who is an expert in the service they offer.

Conclusion

I wrote this book to help educate everyone who walks, rides, cycles, and drives on roads, but especially drivers—to help them become safer drivers, and ultimately, to save lives. Most drivers begin with only the most basic skills and knowledge. Many don't attend driving school—they may learn from others who have little experience and knowledge themselves. Then they are on their own, even though they are not truly ready to be safe and confident drivers.

I wrote this book also to help the driving public be aware of potential dangers; to educate vehicle owners about maintaining their vehicles properly to make them last longer and function more reliably; and to share tips on saving money on repairs and car insurance.

I've also covered tips on how to choose and inspect a vehicle for purchase; how to be sure both you and your vehicle are ready before you set out on a trip of any length; techniques and principles of safe driving;

adapting to changing road and weather conditions; dealing with accidents and breakdowns.

Many of the skills and abilities required to be a good driver can be compared to the skills and strategies required in a game of chess: Knowing yourself and your vehicle; being aware of other drivers, conditions, and surroundings; anticipating and being able to deal with the unexpected.

That's why understanding chess can help you become a better driver. But while chess is only a game, driving a 3,500 pound mobile missile is no game at all; it's serious business. Employing these tips and strategies as you drive may save your life or the life of another, and contribute to safer, more pleasurable motoring.

Note: Before you drive a newly-purchased vehicle, it is vital that you first read the vehicle owner's manual. If on any topic the vehicle owner's manual or your provincial/state driver's manual disagrees with this booklet, then <u>the manual</u> should prevail.

www.ingramcontent.com/pod-product-compliance
Lightning Source LLC
Chambersburg PA
CBHW071546080526
44588CB00011B/1818